EDGE BOOKS™

DRAWING COOL STUFF

HOW TO DRAW

TERRIFYING

ROBOTS

by Aaron Sautter

illustrated by Jason Knudson

Capstone

Mankato, Minnesota

Edge Books are published by Capstone Press,
151 Good Counsel Drive, P.O. Box 669, Mankato, Minnesota 56002.
www.capstonepress.com

Library of Congress Cataloging-in-Publication Data
Sautter, Aaron.
    How to draw terrifying robots / by Aaron Sautter; illustrated by Jason Knudson.
    p. cm.—(Edge Books. Drawing cool stuff)
    Summary: "Lively text and fun illustrations describe how to draw terrifying
robots"—Provided by publisher.
    Includes bibliographical references and index.
    ISBN–13: 978-1-4296-0080-4 (hardcover)
    ISBN–10: 1-4296-0080-2 (hardcover)
    1. Robots in art—Juvenile literature. 2. Fantasy in art—Juvenile literature. 3.
Drawing—Technique—Juvenile literature. I. Knudson, Jason. II. Title. III. Series.
NC825.R56S28 2008
743'.89629892—dc22   2007002915

Credits
Jason Knudson, designer

1 2 3 4 5 6 12 11 10 09 08 07

TABLE OF CONTENTS

WELCOME!

You probably picked this book because you like robots. Or maybe you picked it because you like to draw. Whatever the reason, get ready to dive into the world of robots!

Robots can be big or small, fast or slow, friendly or mean. They can be many shapes and sizes. They can fight, fly, spy, and do many other amazing things. The possibilities are endless.

This book is just a starting point. Once you've learned how to draw the amazing, terrifying robots in this book, you can start drawing your own. Let your imagination run wild, and see what sort of fantastic robots you can create!

4

To get started, you'll need some supplies:

1. First you'll need drawing paper. Any type of blank, unlined paper will do.

2. Pencils are the easiest to use for your drawing projects. Make sure you have plenty of them.

3. You have to keep your pencils sharp to make clean lines. Keep a pencil sharpener close by. You'll use it a lot.

4. As you practice drawing, you'll need a good eraser. Pencil erasers wear out very fast. Get a rubber or kneaded eraser. You'll be glad you did.

5. When your drawing is finished, you can trace over it with a black ink pen or thin felt-tip marker. The dark lines will really make your work stand out.

6. If you decide to color your drawings, colored pencils and markers usually work best. You can also use colored pencils to shade your drawings and make them more lifelike.

5

THE BOB-v2.5

Danger! Danger! The BOB-v2.5 isn't fast. And he doesn't carry any weapons. But he's very loyal and always warns you when trouble is near. After all, once a best friend—always a best friend!

STEP 1

After drawing this robot, try giving him some legs to walk on. He won't get very far without them!

STEP 2

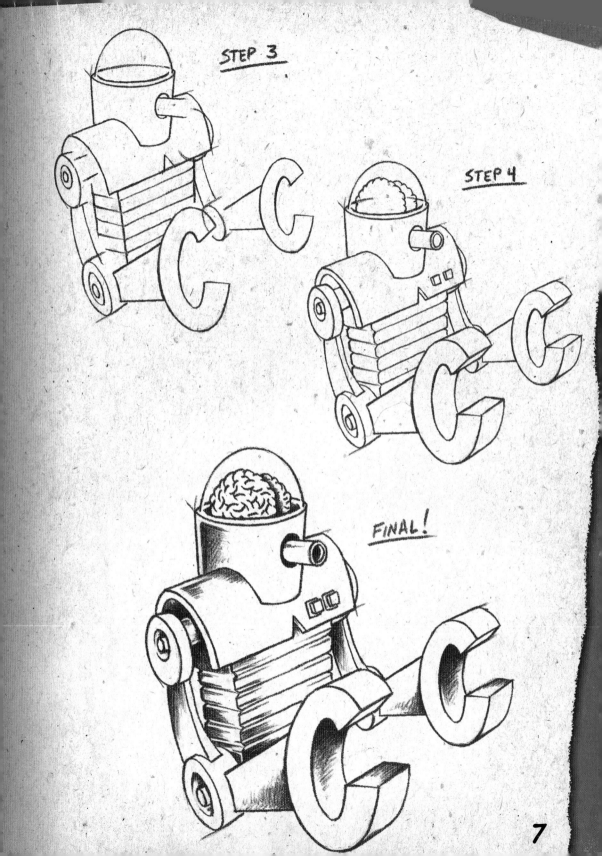

STEP 3

STEP 4

FINAL!

7

MECH-TROOPERS

Mech-Troopers were designed to keep the streets safe from crime. But they soon began keeping the peace by forcing people to stay in their homes. Now everyone hopes the central command unit will be destroyed so people can live their lives in freedom again.

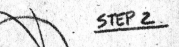
After drawing this robot, try drawing a bunch of them patrolling a city street!

STEP 1

STEP 2

STEP 3

STEP 4

FINAL!

9

THE FXR-UPR

Don't have time for pesky chores? Get yourself the new FXR-UPR! This little robot can do any job with its wide variety of arm attachments. But be sure to keep an eye on it. The FXR-UPR has been known to reprogram itself and destroy its owner's home.

When you're done with this robot, try adding some crazy tools on its arms!

STEP 1

STEP 2

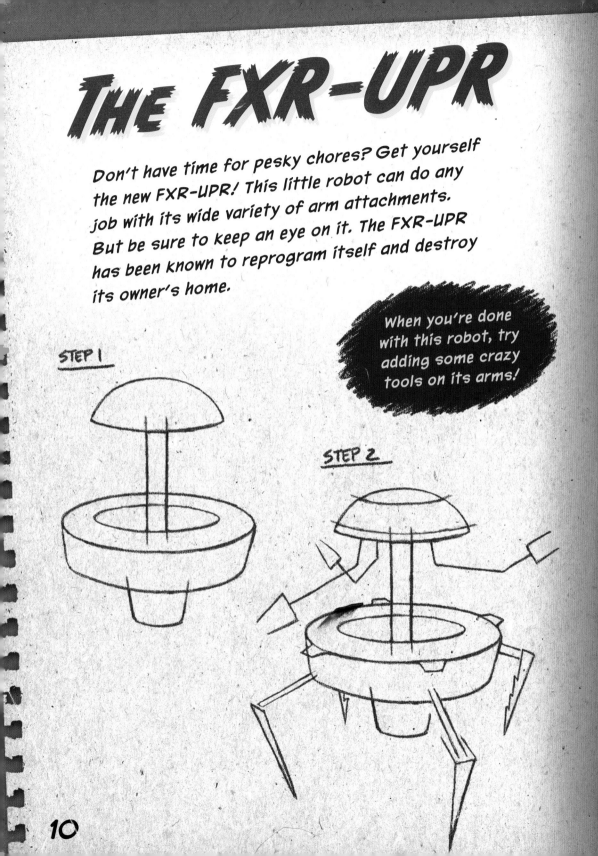

10

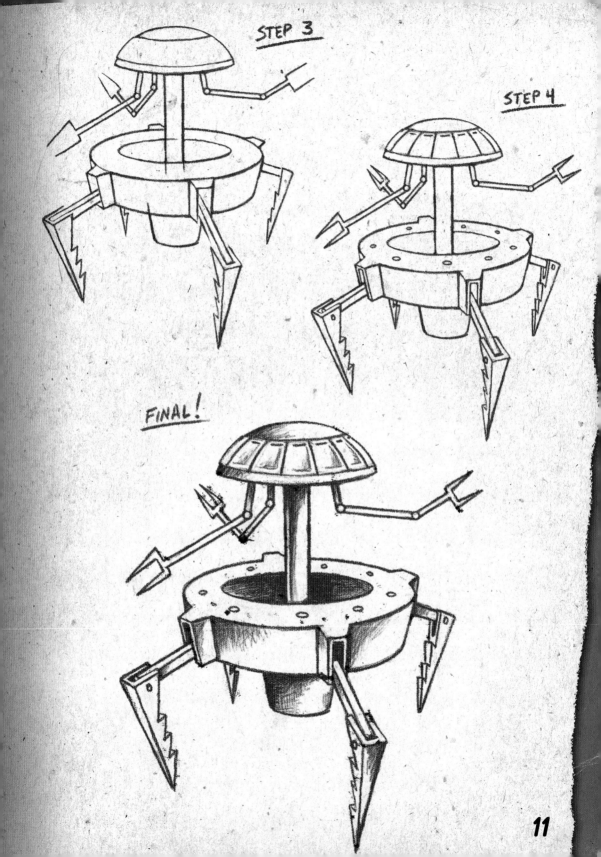

STEP 3

STEP 4

FINAL!

11

THE ECHO-4000

No secret is safe with the ECHO-4000 around. It may look harmless, but it can easily capture and decode your most secret messages. Be careful what you say when one of these is nearby!

When you've learned to draw this robot, try adding some even bigger, crazier antennas!

STEP I

STEP 2

STEP 3

STEP 4

FINAL!

13

THE TENTACLE TERROR X-22

The Tentacle Terror X-22 is slippery and quick. Its twisting, snakelike arms are lightning fast. Be careful! It can snatch you up and carry you off before you know what's happening!

STEP 1

After you've practiced drawing this robot, try it again with even more long, crazy tentacles!

STEP 2

BIO-SCOUT MK5

The planet Thorgo is a barren place. There is little food or water there. The Thorgons created the Bio-Scout MK5 model to search the galaxy and gather new resources. These mechanical menaces have stripped many worlds of all life. Find a good place to hide if you see one of these!

When you're done with this robot, try it again as it stuffs its cargo bay with all sorts of plants and animals.

STEP 1

STEP 2

STEP 3

STEP 4

FINAL!

17

PACIFIER P-17s

In the year 2432, civil war rocks the planet Venus. Pacifier P-17s were created to bring peace. But the machines don't know friend from foe. They crush anyone in their way with their giant mechanical claws.

Once you've practiced this robot, try giving it other kinds of scary mechanical arms!

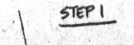

STEP 1

STEP 2

STEP 3

STEP 4

FINAL!

19

THE JET DEFENDER-7

Look! Is that a rocket? No, it's the new Jet Defender-7! It can travel thousands of miles in just seconds with its rocket-powered feet. Don't break the law, or you might be the next one it throws in prison.

After you've practiced this robot, try giving him a partner to help keep the peace around the world!

STEP 1

STEP 2

STEP 3

STEP 4

FINAL!

21

RAMPAGE-XT3

Rampage-XT3 has been seen in many cities in Asia. This giant robot can take the shape of a bulldozer, a tank, or even a jet plane. It can show up anywhere, at any time. But it's easy to follow due to the path of destruction it always leaves behind.

After drawing this robot, try it again as it transforms into a truck, plane, or any other vehicle you can imagine!

STEP 1

STEP 2

22

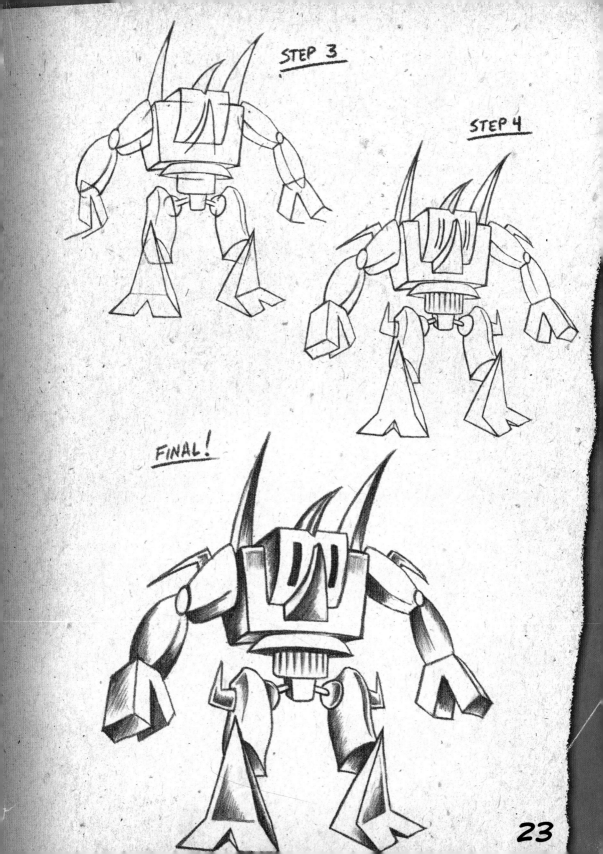

STEP 3

STEP 4

FINAL!

23

THE BUZZ-BOT 6

The giant Buzz-Bot 6 from the planet Praxis-2 has many weapons to use. Deadly spikes cover its arms for defense. And its huge, razor-sharp pincers can easily rip through the thickest armor. Don't make this thing angry, or you'll be sorry!

After you've practiced this robot, try using it in the Robot Rumble on page 26!

STEP 1

STEP 2

STEP 3

STEP 4

FINAL!

ROBOT RUMBLE!

Don't get stuck between Turbo-X and the Morph-Bot 17. When they are locked in full battle mode, you wouldn't stand a chance. Keep clear, or you might find yourself crushed, ripped apart, or burned to a crisp. Let them duke it out, and be sure to make friends with the winner!

After drawing this battle, try it again with any of the robots in this book or from your own imagination!

STEP 1

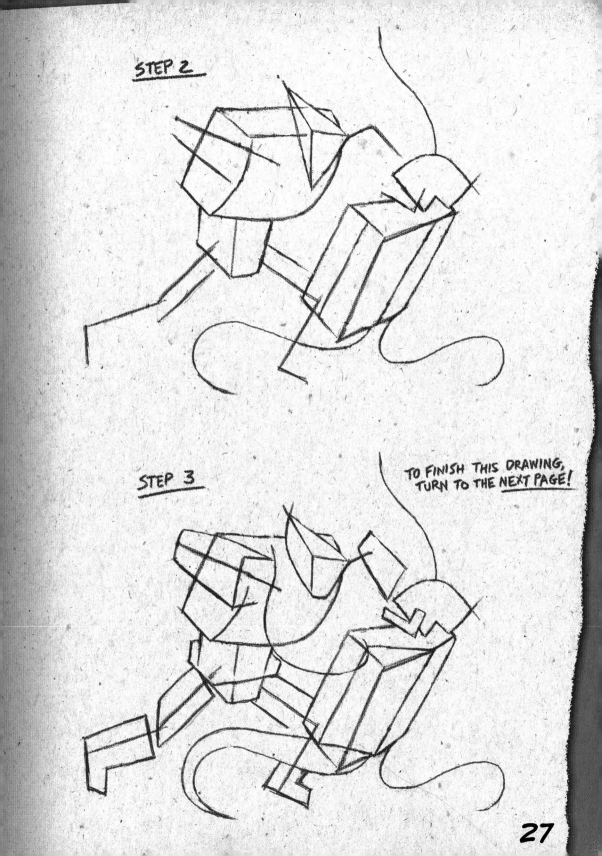

STEP 2

STEP 3

TO FINISH THIS DRAWING,
TURN TO THE NEXT PAGE!

27

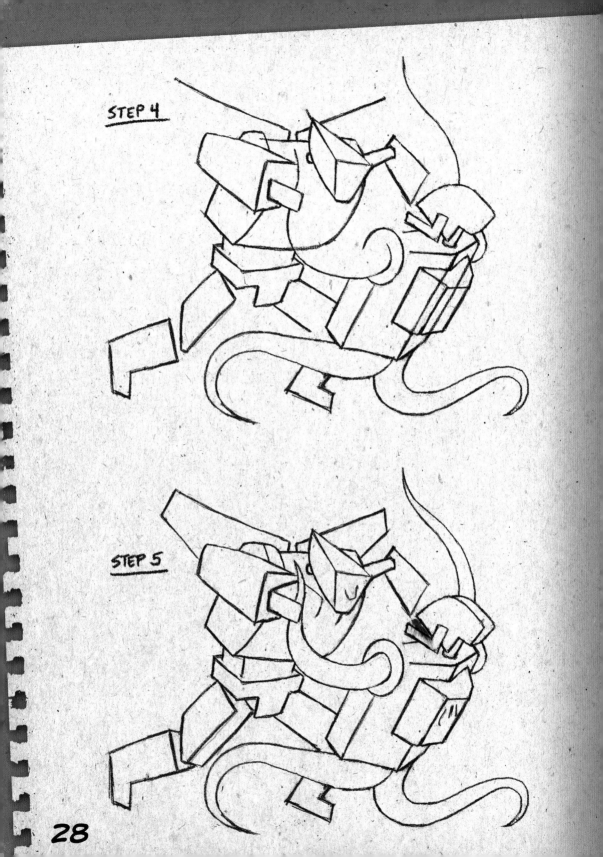

STEP 4

STEP 5

28

STEP 6

FINAL!

GLOSSARY

antenna (an-TEN-uh)—a wire or dish that sends or receives radio waves

cargo bay (KAR-goh BAY)—the area in a vehicle where objects are stored and carried

decode (dee-KODE)—to turn something that is written in code into ordinary language

mechanical (muh-KAN-uh-kuhl)—having to do with machines or tools

menace (MEN-iss)—a threat or danger

patrol (puh-TROHL)—to walk or travel around an area to protect it or to keep watch

pincer (PIN-sur)—a claw used to grasp, hold, or rip apart

reprogram (REE-proh-gram)—to rewrite the set of instructions that tells a computer or machine what to do

tentacle (TEN-tuh-kuhl)—a long, armlike body part used to grab objects

READ MORE

Cook, Janet, and Judy Tatchell. *How to Draw Robots and Aliens.* London: Usborne Books, 2006.

Gray, Peter C. *Robots.* Drawing Manga. New York: PowerPlus Books, 2006.

Stephens, Jay. *Robots! Draw Your Own Androids, Cyborgs and Battle Bots.* New York: Lark Books, 2008.

INTERNET SITES

FactHound offers a safe, fun way to find Internet sites related to this book. All of the sites on FactHound have been researched by our staff.

Here's how:
1. Visit *www.facthound.com*
2. Choose your grade level.
3. Type in this book ID code **1429600802** for age-appropriate sites. You may also browse subjects by clicking on letters, or by clicking on pictures and words.
4. Click on the **Fetch It** button.

FactHound will fetch the best sites for you!   **31**

INDEX

new
2008-09